Afrika Korps
in action

by Bruce Culver
illustrated by Ron Volstad

squadron/signal publications

ISBN 0-89747-079-6

If you have any photographs of the aircraft, armor, soldiers or ships of any nation, particularly wartime snapshots, why not share them with us and help make Squadron/Signal's books all the more interesting and complete in the future. Any photograph sent to us will be copied and the original returned. The donor will be fully credited for any photos used. Please send them to: Squadron/Signal Publications, Inc., 1115 Crowley Dr., Carrollton, TX 75011-5010.

Variant of Afrikakorps cuff title.

AFRIKAKORPS

Officer's block pattern cuff title of "Hermann Göring" division.

HERMANN GÖRING

Isolated in the vast flat expanse of the Libyan desert, the crew of this SdKfz 231 armored car services the 2cm KwK 38 main armament. Because of the destructive effect of the desert sand, most weapons and vehicles had to be maintained and cleaned very carefully. While the crew are all wearing the same type of tropical uniform, this photo shows the noticeable variations in the colors of the cloth. [National Archives]

The Deutsches Afrikakorps

When, in mid-1940, the German OKH (Army High Command) first considered sending an expeditionary force to North Africa to attack British possessions there, including Egypt and the Suez Canal, they could not have guessed that the result of this German intervention in Africa would become one of the most famous military formations in history: The Deutsches Afrikakorps.

The campaign in Africa really begins with the Italian invasion of Ethiopia in 1935. With the advantage of modern weapons, Italy managed to defeat the troops of Haile Selassie and occupied most of the country. With the surrender of France on 22 June 1940, the only country left to resist Germany was England. While the Germans began planning the invasion of Britain - and several alternate plans - the Italians began preparations in their North African colony of Libya for an invasion of Egypt. It was decided that Germany would provide armor support for an Italian campaign against Egypt, and it was hoped that the African action would be over by Autumn 1941.

General von Thoma was sent to Africa to assess the situation for combat operations. His report was pessimistic in view of the difficulties of the poor terrain, lack of transport and port facilities, the questionable effectiveness of the Italian forces, and the limited force (one Panzer Division) that Hitler was considering as an expeditionary army. Hitler nonetheless insisted that this small force would be sufficient, but the unannounced Italian invasion of Greece enraged him and for a time, the Libyan campaign was postponed. Ironically, some Germans later would claim that the need for German troops to rescue the Italians in Greece caused fatal delays in the invasion of Russia.

With the proviso that the Italians make definite progress in invading Egypt, Hitler still intended to commit air units for the support of Italian forces, and ordered the Army to keep a Panzer Division in reserve for possible use in Africa.

These precautions - and the preliminary planning necessary - were well-taken, for the Italians made minimal progress against the British in Egypt. Then on 10 December 1940, the British launched a major counteroffensive against the Italian forces. In one week, the gains of months were lost - the Italians were driven west from Egypt into Libya, and lost over 25,000 men, several generals, and hundreds of vehicles. It was obvious that immediate assistance by Germany was necessary to avoid a complete collapse of the African campaign and the loss of Libya. The Germans wanted to keep Britain fighting in the Mediterranean to draw men and equipment away from any buildup at home.

The German plans for an armored force now included primarily anti-tank

Italian L3 tankettes lead an attack by advancing Italian forces near Adigrat, Ethiopia, 1938. The initial Italian successes in Ethiopia led to a threat to the British positions in Egypt, and after the capitulation of France in June 1940, the conflict spread from the Ethiopian and Libyan theaters. [Bundesarchiv]

guns, pioneer units with mines, and a small unit of PzKpfw III tanks as a mobile force. Flak units were to provide defense against British aircraft. The loss of Tobruk in late January 1941 created a grave crisis, and the timetable was moved up - advance detachments of the 5th leichte Division sailing from Naples at the end of January. As commander, Hitler chose Generalleutnant Erwin Rommel, formerly in charge of Hitler's personal bodyguard, and a veteran of several armor battles as commander of 7th Panzer Division during the invasion of France. Rommel, with a small staff, arrived in Libya on 12 February 1941, and two days later, the first German troops arrived in Tripoli.

It should be understood that the Deutsches Afrikakorps (DAK) always consisted of only two divisions: 5th leichte (light) Division and 15th Panzer

Division. In mid-August 1941, Rommel's African command was expanded to a Panzergruppe ("Panzergruppe Afrika") and included the DAK (21st Panzer Division - formerly the 5th leichte Division - and 15th Panzer Division) plus the 90th leichte Division and six Italian divisions in two corps. Thus, by mid-1941, the DAK had become only a part of a much larger force. The Allies - in the popular press - referred to all the German troops in Africa as the "Afrikakorps," which has no doubt contributed to the fame of this unit. 1941 saw the British driven eastward into Egypt, and the unsuccessful siege of the fortress at Tobruk, which the British had captured from the Italians.

In January 1942, "Panzergruppe Afrika" was reorganized as "Panzerarmee Afrika", also referred to as the "deutsch-italienische Panzerarmee". It then consisted of the DAK, 90th leichte Division, 164th Infanterie Division, the Ramcke Fallschirmjäger (Paratroop) Brigade, three Italian corps (X, XX, XXI) comprising 8 divisions, including two armored units ("Ariete" and "Littorio"), plus dozens of individual units of regimental, battalion, or even company strength, assigned as needed to the groups that requested them. Among these were the Luftwaffe Flak regiments that provided many of the Panzerarmee's antitank units, the artillery command that provided artillery support, a special force (Sonderverband 288) known by the popular name, "Brandenburg" - used in much the same way as the British S.A.S. and L.R.D.G. long-range reconnaissance and raiding groups - and many other support units for water, fuel, transportation, food, etc. 1942 saw the height of German successes in Africa as Tobruk fell on the second try, and the British retreated deep into Egypt, only managing to stop the Germans at Alamein.

In October 1942, the great British offensive began at Alam Halfaya (second battle of Alamein), and the exhausted and poorly supplied German and Italian forces were driven westward into Libya, suffering heavy losses in men and vehicles. During this battle, the Ramcke Brigade, cut off behind British lines, made a forced march to the west to save themselves. During their retreat, the Brigade came upon a supply column for a British armored division camped for the night, and without firing a shot managed to steal the trucks, becoming a motorized unit in the process and bringing back to "Panzerarmee Afrika" transport vehicles and badly needed supplies. It was one of the few bright spots in a retreat that would end 6 months later with the capitulation of all Axis forces in Africa. Rommel, now a Generalfeldmarschall, regrouped his depleted units in Tunisia.

Late 1942 saw the Anglo-American landings in French Morocco (Operation "Torch") and the formation of a new German command in Tunisia to block the eastward advance of the "Torch" forces. This became Panzer Armeeoberkommando 5 (PzA.O.K.5), which comprised 10th Panzer Division (transferred from France), "Division von Broich" (later named "Division von Manteuffel"), Luftwaffe flak units, and later, "Hermann Göring" division ("Kampfgruppe Schmid"), schwerer Panzer Abteilung 501, 21st Panzer Division (detached from the DAK), 334th Infanterie Division, and other support units.

In early 1943, the last units of "Panzerarmee Afrika" entered Tunisia. In February, "Panzerarmee Afrika" was renamed "1. Italienische Armee", and a new high command structure, "Heeresgruppe Afrika", was set up combining PzA.O.K.5 and "1. Italienische Armee". In March, Rommel - who had been ill for some time - left Africa for the last time, Generaloberst von Arnim succeeding him as commander of "Heeresgruppe Afrika".

The final months of fighting were characterized by desperate shortages of fuel, food, and equipment. Unknown to the Germans, the Allies had broken the most secret German codes, and many supply convoys were sunk as a result of this knowledge. As the Allied forces advanced from east and west, the Germans were forced to direct their available forces to meet individual crises. While still capable of dealing crippling blows to the Allies (especially the inexperienced Americans) as veterans of Faid, Kasserine, or Djebel Bou Aoukaz can testify, each battle cost the "Heeresgruppe Afrika" units irreplaceable men, vehicles, and fuel. The Allies could replace their losses in Africa, the Axis could not. A last desperate attempt to reinforce the Tunisian units by air led to the famous "Palm Sunday Massacre" resulting in the loss of dozens of aircraft and hundreds of men. Old units ceased to exist as they were broken up to form dozens of temporary battle groups and defensive units, and most of the divisions that did remain were reduced to little more than regimental strength.

On 12 May 1943, Generaloberst Jurgen von Arnim surrendered all the remaining Axis forces in Tunisia. Nearly 70 tanks were capable of fighting, but lack of fuel stranded them in place, and as the last rounds of ammunition were fired, the crews destroyed their vehicles. Lack of food and other supplies were also critical, and von Arnim later was to claim that the Germans in Tunisia would have had to surrender or starve. Nonetheless, the German troops in Tunisia fought bravely, with great determination. Following the example of their most famous commander, Erwin Rommel, they fought a fair, even honorable, war down to the bitter end. Their enemies respected them as much as their allies did, a notable achievement that can be claimed by few armies in the history of modern warfare.

Generalleutnant Erwin Rommel, selected by Hitler to command the German forces in Africa, arrived in Libya and immediately began to gather information on the status of Italian forces and their British opponents. In this later photo, Rommel discusses a battle situation with his staff and an Italian officer. [National Archives]

The first vehicles sent to Africa were not prepared or modified for desert operations. Here, a SdKfz 223 is seen in its "semi-prepared" position, in early Spring 1941. The dark Gray paint is already covered with dust and the tires are protected from the heat by rocks and sandbags. [Bundesarchiv]

Within days of the arrival of the first German units in Tripoli, Rommel ordered his engineers to construct dummy tank superstructures of wood and cloth, and mount them on Volkswagen Kubelwagens. They bore a close resemblance to the kleiner Betehlspanzer I, and were to convince British intelligence that the Germans had arrived with a strong armored force. [Bundesarchiv]

This PzKpfw II is in the headquarters reconnaissance unit of the second abteilung of PzRgt 5, 5th leichte Division. To the left are a SdKfz 253, SdKfz 251/3, and a heavy passenger car. Note that a couple of the men still wear continental field gray uniforms, though this was not usual. The outline white turret numbers have been partially filled in, probably in red. [Bundesarchiv]

[Below Left] This view of an early SdKfz 223 in the Libyan desert, March 1941, shows the use of mud [or sand spread over oil] to cover the dark gray paint. The black jerrycans with white crosses were used for carrying water. Water supplies were not critical, as the Germans had planned in advance for their water needs in North Africa and their preparations resulted in fairly good supplies of water in most units. [Bundesarchiv]

This SdKfz 263 of PzRgt 5, 5th leichte Division, has been camouflaged with a slurry of mud. Note the vehicle is parked in a shallow pit. This was intended to lower the silhouette somewhat and also to protect the tires. Often during midday, cloth covers were stretched over the wheels to shield them from direct sunlight. Like most other vehicles in the desert, this radio car has a good deal of extra crew stowage. [Bundesarchiv]

The 8.8cm Flak 18, seen here behind a SdKfz 8 12-tonne tractor, was Rommel's "secret weapon" in the early stages of the African campaign. Designed as a dual-purpose weapon for both antiaircraft and ground targets, it proved to be the finest antitank weapon of the African campaign. General Rommel used these guns to destroy British armor at long range after using his own armor to draw out the enemy tanks. Following the Flak 18 is a Krupp Kfz 69 "Protze" light truck. [Bundesarchiv]

1942 pattern "Jerry Can" for water.

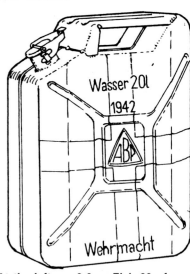

At the left, an 8.8cm Flak 36 of an antitank battery covers a section of coastal road in Libya as a second gun is towed past to its own position. Most "88s" were fired from prepared positions which allowed the guns to be set as low as possible, and afforded a measure of protection for the crews from counterbattery fire. The only major difference between the Flak 18 and Flak 36 was the barrel construction, the Flak 36 having a 3-piece liner which was easier to replace when necessary. [Bundesarchiv]

Several DAK soldiers examine a British A13 Cruiser tank, destroyed in an early engagement in 1941. Many early British tanks were plagued with various mechanical difficulties and their relatively thin armor could be penetrated at very long ranges by the 8.8 cm gun. [Bundesarchiv]

[Above Right] A Flak 18 fires against British vehicles, the muzzle blast sending clouds of dust into the air. The dust was an obvious target for return fire, yet because the "88" was so effective against the earlier British tanks at such long range, the dust of firing often went unnoticed in the smoke and confusion. Often fairly extensive earthworks and trenches were prepared, as seen here. Note the five "kill rings" around the barrel of the gun. [Bundesarchiv]

A destroyed column of British armor near Tobruk, May 1941. The tank is an A13 Cruiser from the 2nd Armoured Division, and the others are two Marmon-Harrington Mk II armored cars. These vehicles were destroyed during the first, unsuccessful attack on the British-held fortress. [Bundesarchiv]

Many areas of the desert presented the same appearance and problems as the sea, vast expanses of flat or slightly undulating, shifting sand, often [as here] with no identifiable landmarks. Navigation was by compass, star and sunsightings, and use of special navigation and surveying instruments like the theodolite. Here, a PzKpfw IB and a PzJag IB support the advance of DAK infantry in the background.

[Below Left] While water supplies were not critical, its transportation was a problem. Since the Afrikakorps was not supplied with tank trucks or water trailers, almost all water had to be carried in the 20 litre jerrycans. At this stage there was no difference between gasoline and water jerrycans, so the painted cross was used to distinguish the containers and prevent cross contamination. [Bundesarchiv]

One area of concern among German units was the establishment of proper rations. The earliest DAK troops had to use predominately Italian rations as the German European rations of potatoes and bread were considered perishable in the African climate. Jaundice and dysentery resulted from the lack of fresh food, and German field bakeries were hastily transferred in March to provide white bread. Here loaves are being stored in the sun. [Bundesarchiv]

German infantry advance during part of the initial assault on Tobruk. In the foreground are several MG 34 teams. Most of these troops wear the breeches and high canvas boots used in Africa, but one man at the right wears the long pants worn outside the boots. Shorts were banned in combat areas because cuts from the rocks and sand did not heal properly, resulting in open sores. [Bundesarchiv]

Desert style boot

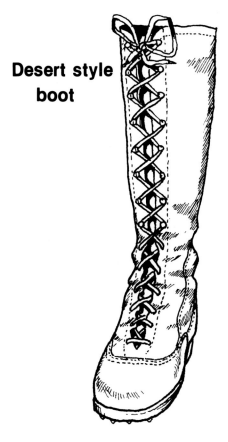

German pioneers climb onto a PzKpfw IV D to ride up to the British positions near Tobruk. Note the use of cloth covers on the helmets and the extra water bottles for each man. The canvas boots were designed for the desert, as leather boots tended to dry out and crack in the heat. [Bundesarchiv]

11

In the early morning and evening, the desert could be fairly cold. These crewmen of a 15 cm sFH18 wear the African issue greatcoats. The caps are much lighter [near white] and may have been bleached deliberately, a common practice. A large national flag has been placed on the hood as an air recognition sign.

[Above Left] This PzJag IB shows how well a heavy coat of dust can cover even the dark gray paint used on early German vehicles. Much of the dust has been rubbed off by the crewmen sitting on top. Though quickly outclassed by the later Matilda infantry tanks, the 4.7 cm Skoda antitank gun of this vehicle was fairly effective against many early British Cruiser tanks and armored cars. These crewmen still wear continental [European] greatcoats. [Bundesarchiv]

Supplies, especially vehicles and fuel, were sometimes critical for much of the African campaign. Here, a SdKfz 6/1 5-tonne artillery tractor is unloaded from a freighter in Tripoli. As the more eastern Libyan ports in Cyrenaica were too shallow for large freighters, vehicles and supplies had to be transported much further, from Tripoli and other ports in the western part of Libya.

This SdKfz 10 of the 21st Panzer Division, seen in late 1941, shows that not all vehicles arrived in Africa painted in the regulation tropical color. A heavy coat of dust, rubbed off many areas, is all that covers the gray European paint scheme. Many DAK vehicles had to be drawn from other formations on short notice and there frequently was no time to paint them before using them in action. [Bundesarchiv]

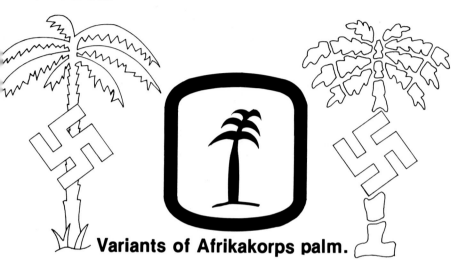

Variants of Afrikakorps palm.

[Below Right] The PzJag IB was another attempt to provide superior antitank capabilities for German troops. This vehicle is being transported on a trailer. Because of the long distances between the major ports and the front lines, most tracked vehicles were shipped by transport trailer or by rail whenever possible, in order to conserve track life.

In order to supplement the limited armament of the earlier models of German tanks, Rommel used the excellent 8.8 cm Flak 18, which he used as close to the front lines as possible. Here, a Luftwaffe "88" travels with a German advance. Most of the heavy flak units were in the Luftwaffe, and because of a shortage of guns, Rommel had to draw some batteries from his airfield defense.

Aerial reconnaissance was very important in the rapid advances and shifting front lines in the desert. Here, Luftwaffe personnel adjust an Rb 50 aerial camera before installing it in the Bf 110 recon fighter behind them. During the African campaign, a number of aircraft were used for reconnaissance duties, including the Bf 110, Fi 156 "Storch", Hs 126 and Fw 189A 'Uhu'. [Bundesarchiv]

[Below Left] The Fieseler Fi 156C "Storch" was one of the most popular and useful liaison aircraft used by the Luftwaffe. It had excellent STOL characteristics and provided excellent vision for the crew. This example, finished in sand with a mottle, probably olive green, displays radio call sign letters rather than a staffel code. Many Storches were used by local cooperation and liaison flights in the DAK. [Bundesarchiv]

All German units in Africa had to adapt to a destructive climate, which made it necessary to alter equipment and perform extra maintenance tasks. This workshop truck and generator trailer were in 2.[H]/14, an Army short range reconnaissance staffel attached to the DAK. A very random spray of sand yellow has been applied over the dark gray base.

Part of any advance in force by the DAK was an antitank detachment, usually equipped with the 8.8 cm Flak 18 or 36, or the 5 cm Pak 38. As was common with desert vehicles, this Sz Kfz 7 carries a huge pile of equipment. The Flak 18 is carried on the earlier type of carriage, the SdAnh 201.

Near Gazala in April 1942, this SdKfz 221 crew uses their vehicle as a forward observation post. The DAK depended very heavily on advance reconnaissance to keep track of enemy movements. Though the 4 wheeled armored cars like this one had only fair crosscountry performance, the firmer expanses of desert were more suitable for wheeled vehicles, and they proved to be very useful in many areas of North Africa. [Bundesarchiv]

A mixed column of German tanks moves toward the front lines. A PzKpfw II aust C leads a PzKpfw IV ausf D and two PzKpfw IIIs. Though the penetration capability of the short howitzer of the PzKpfw IV D was less than the 5 cm L/42 gun of the PzKpfw III, the heavier frontal armor provided enough protection to enable the crews to close to effective range. [Bundesarchiv]

After every successful engagement, the Germans quickly collected all operating British vehicles to supplement their own limited supplies of vehicles. In many respects, British trucks were more suited to the desert than most German types. At one point, Rommel issued an order that all critical supplies [fuel, water, ammunition and food] be carried in British trucks whenever possible. [Bundesarchiv]

[Above Left] Years of preparation and two major aggressive campaigns had given the German armor units priceless experience in tactics. Combined with superior classes of tanks, this experience enabled the DAK to drive the British back through Cyrenaica and inflict heavy losses on British armored units. [Bundesarchiv]

Pith Helmet

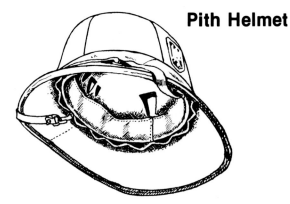

During the initial drive across Cyrenaica, the DAK overran many British positions. This photo shows a British forward aid station which was captured intact with its medical personnel and wounded. The British and German medical personnel later worked together to treat the wounded from both sides. [Bundesarchiv]

The Afrikakorps troops were quick to adopt captured weapons and vehicles to augment their own. Here a captured Marmon-Harrington Mk II armored car has been taken into a German reconnaissance detachment. Note the difference between the narrow tires on the Kubelwagen and the wider type on the armored car. Since the M-H car was painted in a suitable desert color, the Germans have not repainted it. [Bundesarchiv]

[Below Right] Not only trucks but also captured staff cars, like this 1941 Ford, were used by the DAK. Almost all British vehicles were fitted with wide high-flotation tires which proved to be more effective in the desert terrain than the narrow tires used on most German trucks and cars. The windows of this car have been painted to prevent reflected sun flare from disclosing its location, and a water condenser is mounted on the front bumper. [Bundesarchiv]

This Crusader II was destroyed in late 1941. Though relatively fast, the Crusader was not mechanically reliable, and the Mk II did not carry enough armor to stop the 5 cm gun of the PzKpfw III. In addition, a large number of British tanks were destroyed by carefully emplaced antitank guns. [Bundesarchiv]

A number of captured British vehicles were converted for special purposes, largely because of their superior crosscountry performance. This 3-ton Canadian CMP Chevrolet has been fitted with a 2 cm Flak 30, and modified with a Notek light and a rack for German jerrycans. The 1-meter stereoscopic rangefinder shown here was the most common instrument for these light flak guns. [Bundesarchiv]

[Above Left] This captured Chevrolet truck has already been "inducted" into the Luftwaffe, with a new license number, DAK palm, and German flag over the hood as an air recognition sign. Since Ford and Chevrolet also had plants in Germany, German mechanics were able to do routine maintenance on these captured trucks. [Bundesarchiv]

This photo of a German truck column in early 1942 is interesting in that all visible are captured British vehicles. The armored car, a Marmon-Harrington Mk III, retains the original camouflage and a .55 Boys AT rifle and a Bren gun. British armored car crews often appropriated Italian Breda 20 mm cannons and some light machine guns, but here an Italian crew operates this vehicle. [Bundesarchiv]

This PzKpfw III ausf J of PzRgt 8, 15th Panzer Division, was destroyed by British antitank guns in early 1942. Initially a source of maintenance problems, the PzKpfw III later proved to be a reliable and effective vehicle. Until the introduction of the PzKpfw IV ausf F2 with the L/43 gun, the PzKpfw III mounted the most effective tank gun in the African theater, and could knock out most British tanks.

[Above Right] One of the first German tanks to be destroyed and captured was this PzKpfw IV ausf D of PzRgt 5, 5th leichte Division. The yellow-brown paint has been sprayed over the dark gray leaving some gray showing as a mottling. A number of tanks were destroyed by antitank fire and artillery. Shortly, up armored and improved models arrived in Africa, giving a temporary advantage against the standard 2 pdr. British antitank guns.

British troops examine the burning remains of a PzKpfw IV ausf F1 of PzRgt 8, 15th Panzer Division, totally destroyed by internal explosions and fire. The early PzKpfw IV was never available in numbers approaching the total of PzKpfw IIIs but, later in the African campaign, improved PzKpfw IVs were available in much greater quantities.

19

Italian formations comprised a major part of the Axis forces in Italy. Though often forced back in battles with the British, many Italian divisions fought well. They were hampered by inferior weapons and obsolete tanks. This M13/40, 3ª series, of "Ariete" Division was the standard Italian medium tank of the war. While its 47 mm main gun was not a bad weapon, it had a limited effective range. [Bundesarchiv]

Italian Tanker's Helmet

[Below Left] Two tank commanders of 320 R.C., "Ariete" Division, rest during an advance. Note the white crosses on the turret roofs, an air recognition sign. The "VII" identifies the 320 R.C. [tank battalion], the bars indicate company and platoon. [Bundesarchiv]

This M13/40 of "Ariete" Division was typical of Italian medium tanks. It was inferior to most Allied tanks except the early British Cruisers, and in particular, the armor had a tendency to crack or shatter when hit by AP shot; it was not uncommon to find Italian tanks torn apart even by a solid shot. [Bundesarchiv]

A column of M13/40s of the HQ company of the 320 R.C. "Ariete" Division, seen during a halt in the march. These are 2º series vehicles, and have only the front mudguard sections fitted. The color scheme here is probably red brown overall. Because of the low power/weight ratio, the M13/40 was slow and suffered from mechanical breakdowns. [Bundesarchiv]

Italian forces in Africa included a number of detachments of Askari native troops. These two men serve a 7.7 mm Breda aircraft gun adapted for ground use. The Italian native troops served with many other units as combat personnel, airfield guards, and in reconnaissance detachments, where their knowledge of the local terrain and people proved to be valuable. [Bundesarchiv]

This Italian tankette, a CV35[L3] radio vehicle, is missing the antenna. It was part of "Ariete" Division, and belonged to the 2nd platoon of the company. The L3 tankette proved to be vulnerable to virtually all British tanks and armored cars, even armor piercing bullets being capable of penetrating many of the plates. It was designed as a reconnaissance vehicle, but wartime conditions forced the Italians to use it as a light tank, with poor results. [Bundesarchiv]

The L3 tankette was designed for the reconnaissance role, and though it was very vulnerable to enemy fire, it did perform this function adequately. Like the heavier M13/40, the L3 often cracked open when hit by antitank fire, and losses were heavy. Crosscountry performance was not good and the lack of speed resulted in the loss of vehicles which could not outrun enemy units. [Bundesarchiv]

To counteract the introduction of more heavily armored British tanks like the Matilda and Grant, the Germans began sending the DAK more effective antitank weapons. One of the more widely used self-propelled guns was this Russian 76.2mm antitank gun on the chassis of the PzKpfw 38[t]. Though an improvised weapon with a rather high silhouette, the SdKfz 139 was effective and gave the DAK a more effective antitank force. This vehicle, still painted dark gray, has a badly deteriorated coating of dust or mud. [Bundesarchiv]

[Above Left] Early German attempts to mount larger antitank guns on self-propelled carriages included some very crude improvisations. This vehicle, nicknamed "Diana", consisted of a 76.2mm Russian antitank gun mounted, with its carriage, on a 5-tonne Bussing SdKfz 6 artillery tractor. Armor protection against shell splinters was provided by the crude box-shaped armor enclosure. Very few of these were produced, as better mountings soon became available. The Russian gun was very effective, however, and served as an interim weapon until the later introduction of the German 7.5 cm PAK 40.

This vehicle, seen near Tamrad in the Derna area, April 1942, is the 15 cm sIG 33 heavy infantry gun mounted on a modified PzKpfw II chassis. Earlier versions had only 5 roadwheels, but the extra weight and recoil had overloaded the suspension and a 6th wheel was added and the chassis lengthened, which also provided more space for the gun crew. The low armor gave only minimal protection to the crew, but the lack of a higher superstructure made it easier to conceal this vehicle in the desert. [Bundesarchiv]

Because the flat desert terrain gave no protection from shell splinters, infantrymen had to "dig in" at nearly every position. This soldier wears the standard tropical uniform with tropical webbing. The dark waffenferbe around the shoulder boards could be black, indicating this man is a pioneer. The temporary sand coating on his helmet shows the field gray beneath. [Bundesarchiv]

[Above Left] The Germans captured thousands of guns and vehicles during their early campaigns in the West and in the invasion of Russia. Fairly soon, they began to use these weapons as self-propelled guns, and used the vehicles as carriages to mount other armament. This 15cm sFH18 on a French Lorraine tractor chassis, SdKfz 135/1, was used in some numbers in North Africa. Though open at the top, the high superstructure provided better protection than the sIG 33 on the PzKpfw II chassis. This vehicle, captured by the British, is camouflaged in desert brown and dark gray.

Among the more unusual vehicles used by the DAK was this Austrian Saurer RR7 [SdKfz 254] wheel-cum-track armored car. It could be run either as a wheeled vehicle for greater speed or on tracks for better crosscountry performance. This vehicle crew is changing a tire destroyed by a mine. Note the blown out casing and shredded inner tube. The SdKfz 254 was complex and not many were used in North Africa. Eventually it proved more efficient to build better wheeled or tracked vehicles as needed for specific uses. [Bundesarchiv]

Though many Luftwaffe 8.8cm guns were used by Rommel to advance with DAK formations as an antitank force, others had to be left in reserve to protect the airfields so that critically needed supplies could be flown in from Italy and Sicily. Here a Flak 18 crew replaces the barrel on their gun using a Ford 3-tonne truck crane to align the barrel guides with the carriage. The barrel linings had to be replaced periodically as worn liners affected accuracy. In the background is a Bf 110 of ZG26 "Horst Wessel". [Bundesarchiv]

Askari private with standard Italian Sahariana tunic and cloth puttees. He is carrying a Beretta 3A 9mm SMG.

Italian tanker wears a double breasted leather coat with the standard leather tanker's helmet over blue coveralls.

Bersaglieri cyclist wearing an olive green drill tunic. The leather gaiters and cock feathers in the sun helmet were characteristic as was the wearing of the goggles to the side.

Luftwaffe Leutnant wearing the pullover tropical shirt, summer service cap and short leather boots.

General Feldmarschall Erwin Rommel prepares to fly to Italy, putting on a fighter pilot's life vest. He is wearing a custom-made brown uniform with standard European service cap and English goggles.

Machine Gunner, Panzer-
grenadiers wearing a faded
tropical tunic, puttees and
short boots. His helmet and
gas mask can have been
painted desert sand.

Hauptmann, Artillery wearing a custom made olive
green canvas uniform with
officer's high boots.

Gunner's Assistant, Pan-
zergrenadiers wears rela-
tively new olive green tropical tunic and breeches with
one DAK cuff title. Also, he
is wearing the canvas and
leather desert boots.

Obergefreiter, Infantry dug
in wearing the green tropical overcoat with the canvas webbing and brown
ammo pouches. His helmet
has been camouflaged
with tan canvas

Leutnant, Panzertroops
wears the European style
black panzer cap, preferred
by tank crews to the peaked
cap. His tunic collars bear
both the standard army-style
collar bars and aluminum
Totenkopf pins.

The flat expanses of the Western Desert made concealment difficult and both sides used forward outposts to provide the earliest possible warning of enemy movements. Here, two men use a spotting telescope in an outpost dug out of a rocky outcropping. They will report their sightings by radio to their headquarters. Often tarpaulins or blankets were stretched over these emplacements as camouflage and shade from the sun. [Bundesarchiv]

[Above Right] Communications, always important to the military, were especially useful to the DAK because of the great distances involved in the rapid movement of the desert campaign. Here are seen three of the standard communications and reconnaissance vehicles: a standard motorcycle and sidecar, Kfz 15 radio truck, and a SdKfz 263 armored radio car. These vehicles are attached to 15th Panzer Division. [Bundesarchiv]

Side Cap

Field Cap

This late production Kfz 15 passenger car serves as a mobile radio station, using a lightweight radio [Torn.Fu.bl] to relay messages. This crew has been assigned to monitor the local area and report changes in the situation to the main unit. Note the canvas windshield cover to prevent reflected glare from revealing the location of the car. [Bundesarchiv]

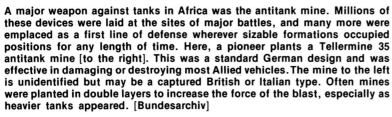

A major weapon against tanks in Africa was the antitank mine. Millions of these devices were laid at the sites of major battles, and many more were emplaced as a first line of defense wherever sizable formations occupied positions for any length of time. Here, a pioneer plants a Tellermine 35 antitank mine [to the right]. This was a standard German design and was effective in damaging or destroying most Allied vehicles. The mine to the left is unidentified but may be a captured British or Italian type. Often mines were planted in double layers to increase the force of the blast, especially as heavier tanks appeared. [Bundesarchiv]

[Above Right] Though the German units in Africa were continuously short of supplies, replacements and better equipment did arrive. Here, a PzKpfw III ausf L is seen in 1942. The later desert brown was a very deep tan-brown and often photographs nearly as dark as dark gray. The 5cm Kwk 39 L/60 was capable of penetrating most Allied tanks used in Africa, and until more long-barreled PzKpfw IVs were available, the PzKpfw III had to bear the brunt of the antitank fighting in the Panzer Divisions. [Bundesarchiv]

Later replacement vehicles to the DAK were more properly prepared for shipment and tropical service before they left Europe. This SdKfz 222 light armored car being unloaded in Africa has been painted in desert brown, and has a new dust fitter, seen behind the turret, on the hull. Like many vehicles, this one carries boxes of spares and equipment on the engine deck. [Bundesarchiv]

This SdKfz 232 [8 rad] armored car shows some of the modifications made by DAK personnel to make their vehicles more suitable for desert use. Extra tires have been piled on the engine deck and strap steel frames fabricated to hold 20 litre jerrycans of water. Many parts of the Western Desert had a good deal of sharp stones below the sand surface, and this combined with heat and mines, made provision of extra spare tires a wise move. [Bundesarchiv]

[Above Right] A column of tanks and vehicles of PzRgt 8, 15th Panzer Division, passes a roadside marker, early January 1942. The "Wolfsangel" symbol of PzRgt 8 can barely be seen in the right center of the trailer behind the 1-tonne tractor in the foreground. The tractor has a rack for water cans, added by the unit. Often, a unit would alter all their tanks or vehicles with very similar stowage installations. This became a way of identifying a unit. [Bundesarchiv]

In addition to the famous "88", other towed antitank guns were used to support the tanks. For most of the African campaign, the most common and effective antitank gun was the 5 cm PAK 38, developed by Rheinmetall. A development of this gun was the KWK 39, used in the PzKpfw III. The SdKfz 10 1-tonne halftrack was the standard towing vehicle for the PAK 38, and carried the crew and some ammunition. [Bundesarchiv]

The 15 cm sFH 18 was the standard German medium field gun. Here, one is being towed by an SdKfz 7 tractor near Gazala in April 1942. For long distances, the barrel was disconnected from the recuperator system and carried in full recoil position to shorten the gun and make it easier to negotiate sharp corners in built up areas. [Bundesarchiv]

A radio detachment was assigned to field gun batteries to relay orders and target information. This is a Kfz 15 radio truck, one of several special types used in North Africa. This unit was near Gazala in April 1942. [Bundesarchiv]

One step in the emplacement of a 15cm sFH 18. Here, the trails are lifted off the limber which is then rolled to the side. Next the trail spades will be fitted and the piece will be placed in its prepared position for firing. Note the variety of uniforms found in this crew. Several alternative uniform combinations were possible. [Bundesarchiv]

Here the crew unloads 15cm shells from a truck. Because of the need for protecting the shells from damage, virtually all ammunition was shipped in containers. These woven wicker basket tubes were one of the most common types in the desert. [Bundesarchiv]

[Above Right] The 15cm sFH 18, like many larger artillery pieces, used separate ammunition, the propellant charge was separate from the projectile. Usually several different charges were provided, for using different types of shells which did not have similar weights, or for achieving different maximum ranges with each type of shell. The men on the left are stacking metal propellant casings. [Bundesarchiv]

The heavy muzzle blast from the 15cm guns raised clouds of dust that could reveal the battery positions. Careful reconnaissance was used to detect any enemy movement of artillery or armor that might signal an attack against this position. The gun crews had little protection from sustained counterbattery fire. [Bundesarchiv]

The "Desert Fox", General der Panzertruppe Erwin Rommel, seen in early 1942. He is riding in a Kfz 15 m.E. Pkw. [medium standard passenger car] of the 15th Panzer Division. Rommel was promoted to Generaloberst on 1 February 1942. He commanded "Panzergruppe Afrika", which consisted of the DAK [15. & 21.P.D.] plus 90th leichte Division and 6 Italian divisions. On 30 January 1942, this command was renamed "Panzerarmee Afrika". [Bundesarchiv]

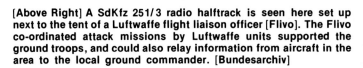

Luftwaffe Cap

[Above Right] A SdKfz 251/3 radio halftrack is seen here set up next to the tent of a Luftwaffe flight liaison officer [Flivo]. The Flivo co-ordinated attack missions by Luftwaffe units supported the ground troops, and could also relay information from aircraft in the area to the local ground commander. [Bundesarchiv]

Sand tables were used for several purposes. Here a reconnaissance detachment is being debriefed, and the results of their mission are plotted on the table. Positions of enemy troops in a village are noted here. Often sand tables were used to plan offensive moves or to direct the emplacement of guns and vehicles. [Bundesarchiv]

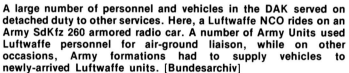

A large number of personnel and vehicles in the DAK served on detached duty to other services. Here, a Luftwaffe NCO rides on an Army SdKfz 260 armored radio car. A number of Army Units used Luftwaffe personnel for air-ground liaison, while on other occasions, Army formations had to supply vehicles to newly-arrived Luftwaffe units. [Bundesarchiv]

[Above Right] Three PzKpfw IIs of PzRgt 8, 15th Panzer Division, pass part of the headquarters staff. The first and last tanks are ausf Cs; the middle one is ausf F. Though outclassed as a combat vehicle by 1941, the PzKpfw II proved to be a useful reconnaissance vehicle, and served through the campaign in Africa. Note the added armor on the nose of the lead vehicle. The original configuration was a single curved plate. [Bundesarchiv]

Elements of PzRgt 5, 21st Panzer Division advance past abandoned British trucks near Acroma during the successful assault on Tobruk, 27 June 1942. Again, a wide variety of uniform combinations can be seen. Shorts were eventually banned for combat troops as leg wounds did not heal well in Africa's climate, and more protection was needed. The PzKpfw II ausf F is from the reconnaissance company, I Abt. PzRgt 5. [Bundesarchiv]

The often rapid and far-ranging shifts in positions resulted in the capture of much material that could not be withdrawn. This is a British 25 pdr field gun, captured in March 1942. If these captured weapons were functioning and sufficient ammunition was available, the Germans quickly adopted them to supplement their own limited numbers of artillery pieces. [Bundesarchiv]

[Above Right] A captured CMP 6 pdr portee, being inspected by DAK personnel. The British 6 pdr [57 mm] was an excellent light-medium antitank gun, and eventually was the basis for the U.S. 57 mm M1 AT gun. This crew has apparently already settled down, with a sunshade and blanket "mattress" next to the truck. [Bundesarchiv]

Another view of the same vehicle, showing the soft-top cab and extra stowage. The strap frames over the front bumper were intended to carry the British-style P.O.W. "flimsy" tins, but a jerrycan could be accommodated as shown. The 20 litre [5 gallon] jerrycan was such an improvement that the Allies began making copies in 1942, which are still in use. In many cases, captured vehicles like this would be modified for German service, fitted with Notek lights and other equipment. [Bundesarchiv]

The 76.2 mm self propelled antitank gun was the heaviest mobile antitank weapon available to the DAK until the introduction of the Marder II in Tunisia. This shot shows its high, narrow silhouette, which was a disadvantage in flat terrain. The gun was modified by removing the lower carriage and adding a muzzle brake.

[Above Right] One of the first US-built medium tanks encountered by the DAK, this British "Grant" was knocked out by 5cm Pak 38s near Bir el Harmat, May 1942. Though the Germans were able to destroy these rather high vehicles, the combination of heavier armament and good armor made them much more difficult targets. This Grant carries an unusual outlined wavy bordered camouflage pattern used by some Grants in the battle of Gazala. [Bundesarchiv]

Another captured Grant, destroyed in June 1942. This vehicle shows the sponson mounting for the 75 mm M2 gun. Though this mounting made it difficult to place the tank in hull-down defensive positions, the 75 mm weapon was the first Allied tank gun in Africa to fire explosive-filled APC ammunition. All 2 pdr and 6 pdr British AT guns fired only solid shot AP ammunition, which often did not destroy a tank even with a direct hit. Also, the 75 mm gun fired an effective HE round which enabled tank crews to destroy emplaced German antitank guns by killing the crews. [Bundesarchiv]

This view of an 8.8cm Flak 18, manned by the operations staff of Panzerarmee Afrika, shows a typical emplacment dug for these weapons. The shallow pit, lined with sandbags, was intended to lower the silhouette, and the scrub brush tied to the shield was to break up its flat shape. Note the metal tubes for the 8.8cm ammunition. These were the most common containers for "88" shells because of the extremes of climate and the sensitivity of the fuses. The tubes were all steel with locking caps containing rubber sealing gaskets. [Bundesarchiv]

[Above Right] Among the many British vehicles destroyed by long range antitank guns was this British "Valentine" infantry tank. Though better armored than most of the Cruiser tanks of the period, the "Valentine" was still vulnerable to the 5cm and 8.8cm German guns. In the background, the desert is littered with knocked out or abandoned British vehicles. [Bundesarchiv]

One of the more unusual vehicles employed by German forces in Africa was the NSU SdKfz 2 Kleines Kettenkrad [KKK], a halftrack tractor developed for airborne use, but in the event, used entirely as a ground vehicle. Though its towing capacity was limited, its good crosscountry performance and high speed made it a very useful vehicle in Africa, and a number of units used them. [Bundesarchiv]

One of the first Luftwaffe units sent to Africa as a combat force was the Ramcke parachute brigade. Originally formed for the invasion of Malta, this formation was sent to Africa as reinforcement after the German advance into Egypt was halted at El Alamein. Here, a reconnaissance patrol operates a Kfz 15 passenger car. The MG34 is mounted on a collapsible anti-aircraft tripod. An Italian colonial trooper [at left] accompanies the Luftwaffe personnel. These native troops provided valuable information on local terrain, possible routes for reconnaissance units to follow, and had a familiarity with local languages and customs that were of great use to the DAK. [Bundesarchiv]

[Above Right] Because the Ramcke brigade was transported by air from Greece, their vehicles had to be drawn from other units in Africa. Here, an Army Kubelwagen carries the famous kite insignia of the Ramcke brigade. Colonial troops watch a Luftwaffe crewman inflate a tire. This vehicle has the large doughnut-shaped balloon tires developed for better flotation in the desert sand. [Bundesarchiv]

Eventually, the brigade received its own vehicles. Here is a brigade Kfz 4 leE.Pkw. [light standard passenger car]. The Kfz 4 was a light antiaircraft vehicle mounting twin MG 34s on a pedestal. It was used as a short to medium range AA weapon. This vehicle is seen in eastern Tunisia, late 1942. The brigade was sent to Tunisia to recuperate from their forced march west from the German lines at Alamein after they were cut off by the British advance. During the retreat, the brigade "appropriated" the vehicles of a British supply column without firing a shot and drove back to the German lines in Libya. [Bundesarchiv]

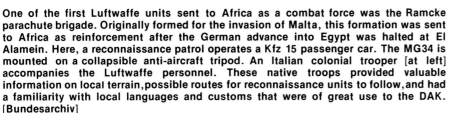

Fuel of German and Italian units was transported to supply depots and most refuelling operations took place at these stations. Here, an Italian Fiat sedan is being refuelled. The supply of jerrycans has been broken into dispersed sections so that a strafing aircraft or an artillery shell wouldn't set off the whole depot. [Bundesarchiv]

3. Panzer Division

10. Panzer Division

15. Panzer Division

21. Panzer Division

A column of Italian armor, seen in Egypt, July 1942. The lead vehicle is a Fiat 508C/1100 military passenger car, the tanks are M13/40s. The Fiat was a standard design used until the end of the war. Though many areas of the desert provided good terrain for tanks, most armored units preferred to remain on the roads as much as possible. [Bundesarchiv]

This M13 "carro commando" [command tank] of "Ariete" division serves as a mobile observation post. The raised stepped observers pole was an improvised fitting, and had the same purpose as a ship's crow's nest: earlier sighting of the enemy. The extra radio antenna was carried by most of these command vehicles. Folded on the glacis of this vehicle is a camouflage net. When stretched over the vehicle, the net would tend to make it appear to be a small hillock or sand dune. [Bundesarchiv]

[Below Right] M13/40s of "Ariete" Division advance in late 1942. "Ariete" was considered one of the best Italian units, and its combat effectiveness was limited mainly by its relatively inferior equipment rather than the caliber of personnel. To compensate for the poor armor protection, these crews have added layers of sandbags to the fronts of their tanks. The always-present dust caused many maintenance problems, even with the later, more advanced protective filters that were devised. [Bundesarchiv]

Units of "Ariete" armored division support an advance west of Bir Hacheim, April 1942. These are Semovente M 40 da 75/18 assault guns, built on the 13/40 chassis. The leading vehicle is an M13 command tank, a standard Italian command vehicle. [Bundesarchiv]

During a field training exercise, reinforcement troops practice tactics for the desert theater. Here, two pioneers of an assault unit carry an MG34 and ammunition; note the black waffenfarbe outlining the shoulder boards. As was common, these men have repainted their field gray helmets with sand colored paint, leaving the uneven appearance seen here. [Bundesarchiv]

[Below Left] Attempting yet another redistribution of wealth, these Luftwaffe troops of "Hermann Göring" division play cards in Tunisia. Their SdKfz 10 tractor has been prepared for tropical use. It may have originally been an Army vehicle. HG was dispatched to North Africa to help hold the line against the Allied landings in Morocco [Operation Torch]. The first units to arrive were attached to 10th Panzer Division which was also transferred from France in late 1942. [Bundesarchiv]

Other units of "Panzerarmee Afrika" were still retreating across Libya in the face of overwhelming enemy strength after the second battle of Alamein. A command halftrack with an improvised perimeter style radio antenna is seen while the crew exchanges information with that of another SdKfz 251/3. The vehicle on the left, also an ausf C, carries on its hood the white transverse air recognition stripe used on many DAK vehicles. [Bundesarchiv]

The retreat into Tunisia had one helpful side effect for the Germans and Italians, the supply lines to Tunisia were shorter than those to Libya. And distances from the main port of Tunis to the front lines also became shorter as the Allies advanced. Here, an M 14/41 is unloaded from a tank transporter trailer. The M 14/41 was a modified version of the M 13/40, differing primarily in having a slightly more powerful engine. [Bundesarchiv]

[Below Right] A new weapon employed by the Italians in Tunisia was this Semovente L40 da 47/32. Based on the chassis of the L6/40 light tank, this small assault gun mounted the same 47 mm antitank gun found in the M 13/40 medium tank. Though outclassed by later developments in armor, it was capable of destroying many Allied armored vehicles, and its low silhouette [5' 8" high] made it easy to conceal in Tunisia's temperate climate with its heavier vegetation and hilly terrain. [Bundesarchiv]

"Panzerarmee Afrika" also received reinforcements in Tunisia. This PzKpfw IV ausf G is part of PzRgt 7, 10th Panzer Division. The PzKpfw IV ausf G was very similar to the F2 variant, mounting an L/43 Kwk 40. This 7.5cm gun was capable of destroying any Allied tank in Africa, and provided a formidable weapon to the Panzer Divisions in Tunisia. For the first time, these long-barreled PzKpfw IVs outnumbered the older models armed with the short howitzer.

Among the reinforcements sent to Africa in late 1942 was sPzAbt. 501 [Tiger]. This heavy tank battalion had two companies of PzKpfw VI "Tiger" ausf E, which were supported by PzKpfw III ausf N tanks mounting 7.5cm L/24 howitzers. This Tiger ausf E has not had the side mudguards fitted and is probably being driven from the railhead to the unit location. The muzzle dust cover was generally used to keep the gun bores clean during transportation. A thick layer of dust had already covered this vehicle, obscuring the battalion symbol on the front plate. [Bundesarchiv]

Feld Bluse

One of sPzAbt. 501's "Tigers" advances to the unit's position, Tunisia, 1942. These early Tigers were fitted with the "Feifel" tropical air filter system, and are typical of early production vehicles. Though very effective against all Allied tanks because of its 8.8cm Kwk 36, ironically many Tigers were lost in Africa because the Spring rains in Tunisia made much of the countryside impassable to tanks of that weight. Forced to stay on roads or higher solid areas, some tanks were destroyed by concealed antitank guns fired from ambush, a reversal of the situation in the Western Desert. [Bundesarchiv]

Elements of the II Abteilung PzRgt 7, 10th Panzer Division travel along a road in the Tunisian foothills. A PzKpfw IV ausf G passes a SdKfz 252 munitions carrier, followed by a PzKpfw II ausf F. The Tunisian country was hilly and very rocky, reminiscent of Sicily and much of central Italy. The temperate climate led to the issuing and use of a good deal of European clothing and equipment. [Bundesarchiv]

[Above Right] This SdKfz 251 ausf C of 10th Panzer Division carries Generaloberst Jurgen von Arnim, the commander of Panzer Armeeoberkommando 5, the German command in Tunisia. Later, with the arrival of all the German and Italian units retreating west from Libya, PzA.O.K.5 was superceded by "Heeresgruppe Afrika" which assumed control over all Axis forces in Africa. [Bundesarchiv]

Vehicles of II Abt, PzRgt 7, 10th Panzer Division prepare for action in Tunisia. PzKpfw IV ausf G and PzKpfw III ausf M tanks were the standard combat types, though the PzKpfw III was by now obsolescent. The effect of the temperate weather can be seen in the heavy coat of mud on the tanks' suspensions. In many areas of this part of North Africa, the spring rain was heavier than some areas of Europe, and the days of hot desert sands were largely over. These replacement vehicles were probably painted in the new dark yellow camouflage color, which proved ideal for the Tunisian campaign. [Bundesarchiv]

Mute testimony to the fury of a German counterattack, this British Humber Mk III armored car of the 6th Armoured Division was blown apart and burned out in eastern Tunisia. On several occasions, German combat groups [Kampfgruppen] staged bold, often successful, local offensives to hold up the Allied advance and enable new lines of resistance to be formed. As the Tunisian campaign progressed, almost all the German armor was incorporated into the many temporary Kampfgruppen that were formed, expended, and replaced by still other specially-formed groups, and many of the basic divisions no longer functioned as complete units. [Bundesarchiv]

Though the Germans and Italians of "Heeresgruppe Afrika" were being pressed on all sides, they were still quite capable of delivering damaging blows to the Allies. Here, a PzKpfw III ausf L, probably of PzRgt 7, 10th Panzer Division, transports British prisoners through a muddy field in Tunisia. The large "7" indicates the company in the regiment, the small "19" below indicates the vehicle number. [Bundesarchiv]

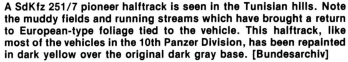

A SdKfz 251/7 pioneer halftrack is seen in the Tunisian hills. Note the muddy fields and running streams which have brought a return to European-type foliage tied to the vehicle. This halftrack, like most of the vehicles in the 10th Panzer Division, has been repainted in dark yellow over the original dark gray base. [Bundesarchiv]

[Above Right] A late production SdKfz 232 [8 rad] radio armored car moves past a burned out Italian Semovente assault gun and a captured, repainted American Jeep. The armored car, followed by a Tiger of sPzAbt 501, is painted dark yellow and has the external mantlet and simplified nose of the later production SdKfz 231 series. The Willys MB Jeep has the slatted radiator grill used only on the first 25,000 Jeeps built. Though the Semovente may have been an Italian vehicle, a great deal of Italian equipment was used to supply "Hermann Göring' division, which arrived without many of its own vehicles.

In the early engagements between German and American units, the US forces learned the same hard lessons in armor tactics the British had learned in the Western Desert a year before, and losses were heavy. The best known American defeat was at Kasserine Pass. After the battle, the Germans retrieved a large number of American vehicles and weapons. This US T19 HMC, originally mounting a 105 mm howitzer, has been converted with an unidentified weapon. A front superstructure roof has been added, as have oversize German markings. The paint scheme is very likely the original US mixture of sand patches on an OD base. [Bundesarchiv]

Comrades in arms - an Italian Semovente L/40 da 47/32 passes SdKfz 233 support vehicle of 10th Panzer Division in Tunisia. Luftwaffe paratroopers were attached to this unit for part of the Tunisian campaign and some of them accompany this vehicle. The SdKfz 233 was developed from the SdKfz 231 armored car, using L/24 short guns no longer needed for PzKpfw IV production. This vehicle also mounts a new MG 42, the successor to the MG 34, which was first used in action in North Africa in 1942. [Bundesarchiv]

sPz Abt 501 Insignia

Here, a captured US M2 halftrack and trailer transport supplies for s PzAbt. 501. The number 501 is seen chalked on the Tiger roadwheel in the trailer. German losses [and the complete breakdown of the supply system], combined with the capture of much Allied equipment, led to the fact that 85% of German vehicles by April 1943 were US or British types. [Bundesarchiv]

Most of "Hermann Göring" division had been transported to Tunisia by March, 1943. Among the forces employed were StuG III assault guns. Here, HG panzergrenadiers jump off a StuG III ausf F/8 during an assault against Allied positions in southern Tunisia. These troops wear European uniforms and equipment. In the final stages of the African campaign, units were dispatched as fast as possible, and tropical equipment was not really necessary in much of Tunisia. [Bundesarchiv]

After 26 February 1943, sPzAbt. 501 was attached to PzRgt 7, 10th Panzer Division as an organic part of the regiment. In practice, members of the unit continued to refer to themselves as sPzAbt. 501 even when the unit was broken up to supply the various Kampfgruppen formed in the last month of the campaign. This Tiger, seen before 501 was incorporated into PzRgt 7, shows very well the tropical Feifel air cleaners. [Bundesarchiv]

Because of the limited number of vehicles, brought into Africa with HG, a good deal of the better Italian equipment was assigned to the Luftwaffe troops. This Semovente M41 da 75/18 was not as well armed as the latest versions of the StuG III, but it was an effective weapon with a low silhouette, and was capable of knocking out many Allied vehicles with special antitank ammunition. Note the Italian helmet on the front plate, indicating that the vehicle was handed directly from an Italian unit to the HG troops. [Bundesarchiv]

On 12 May 1943, Generaloberst Jurgen von Arnim surrendered to the US and British forces. He represented the troops of "Heeresgruppe Afrika" and the DAK, the latter having retained its individual identity even as part of the larger formation. The commander of the DAK, General der Panzertruppe Hans Cramer, sent a final defiant message to "Heeresgruppe Afrika" and the OKH in Germany, which ended by saying that the "Deutsche Afrikakorps must rise again". Hours later, the DAK marched into prison compounds for the rest of the war. [Bundesarchiv]

By the end of April 1943, the end of the fighting in North Africa was clearly in sight. Shortages of fuel, ammunition, vehicles, and men hampered the ability of the German staff of "Heeresgruppe Afrika" to organize effective defenses. As the Germans became weaker, the Allies pressed in with greater effort, and gained ground rapidly. Many German troops, without supplies or equipment to continue to fight, could only wait and watch the Allied forces approaching. [Bundesarchiv]

This blown up PzKpfw IV ausf F2, destroyed in Libya in 1942, is symbolic of the end of the DAK and "Heeresgruppe Afrika". The furious, constant fighting in Tunisia took a great toll of men and machine, but even at the end there were nearly 70 tanks still capable of fighting, if only they had carried fuel for their engines. Unable to move, the majority of these vehicles were destroyed by their crews, or by Allied armor that came across them in exposed positions. Relatively few survived intact to be surrendered to the Allies.